FLAG DAY

by Robin Nelson

first step nonfiction

Lerner Publications Company · Minneapolis

We **celebrate** Flag Day every year.

2009   June

SUNDAY	MONDAY	TUESDAY	WEDNESDAY	THURSDAY	FRIDAY	SATURDAY
	1	2	3	4	5	6
7	8	9	10	11	12	13
14 Flag Day	15	16	17	18	19	20
21	22	23	24	25	26	27
28	29	30				

This holiday is on June 14.

On Flag Day, we **honor** the flag of the United States.

4

The U.S. flag is called the
Stars and Stripes.

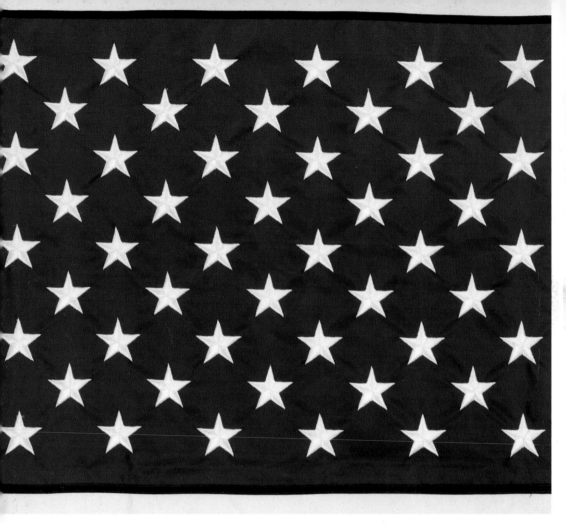

The flag has 50 stars.

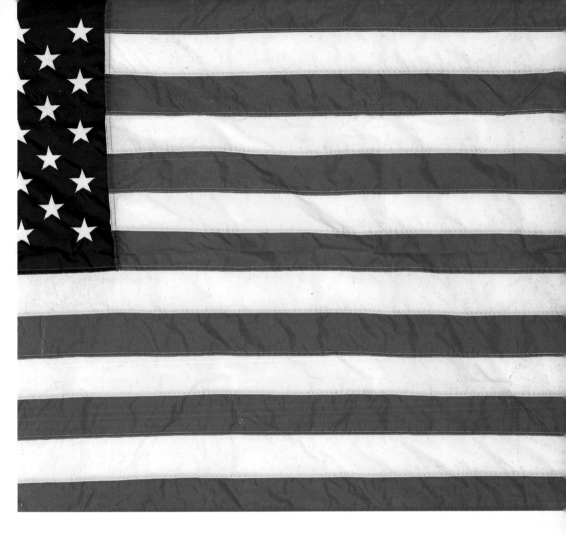

It has 13 red and white stripes.

A teacher had the idea to celebrate our flag's birthday.

He wanted a holiday to
celebrate the flag.

9

Other people celebrated the
U.S. flag's birthday too.

Many years later, Flag Day
became a holiday.

Every year we celebrate
our flag.

We hang flags on our houses.

We fly flags from buildings.

We march in parades with flags.

We see flags everywhere!

We are **proud** of our **country** and flag.

Flag Day Timeline

1776
The first U.S. flag
was created.

June 14, 1877
The U.S. flag's
100th birthday
is celebrated.

June 14, 1777
Leaders made the
"Stars and Stripes"
the U.S. flag.

May 30, 1916
President Wilson asked to make Flag Day a holiday.

June 14, 1885
A teacher in Wisconsin celebrated the birthday of the U.S. flag.

August 3, 1949
President Truman made Flag Day a holiday.

Flag Day Facts

 The 13 stripes—7 red and 6 white—on the U.S. flag stand for the first 13 colonies of the United States of America.

 The 50 stars on the U.S. flag stand for the 50 states in the United States of America.

 The first U.S. flag only had 13 stars.

 A teacher named Bernard C. Cigrand had the idea that Flag Day should be a holiday. He worked his whole life to help make it a holiday for the United States.

The U.S. national anthem, "The Star-Spangled Banner," was written in 1814 by Francis Scott Key. He wrote it after a battle to honor our country and flag.

 There are many rules for taking care of a U.S. flag. Here are some of the rules:

☆ Always fly the flag with the blue part at the top of the pole.

☆ Only fly the flag at night if there is a light shining on it.

☆ Never let the flag touch the ground.

☆ Always fold your flag. Never stuff it in a box or drawer.

Glossary

 celebrate – to have a party or special activity to mark an occasion

 country – a land where people live under one government

 honor – to show special respect for

 proud – feeling happy and respectful about something